2

Milligan's Ark

First edition published November 1971
© M. & J Hobbs
Designed and Produced by Peter Windett
Published by M & J Hobbs, Bridge Street, Walton-on-Thames, Surrey.
Printed by Thomas Nelson (Printers) Limited, Edinburgh.

SBN 85138 917 4

Distributed by Michael Joseph Limited.
52 Bedford Square, London WC1.

MILLIGAN'S ARK

Edited by Spike Milligan and Jack Hobbs

Foreword by HRH. The Prince Philip, Duke of Edinburgh
KG, PC, KT, GMBE, FRS.

Margaret and Jack Hobbs

Acknowledgement
    The editors and publishers would like
to thank all the contributors for their
generosity, and all the other people who
have helped to produce the book,
particularly Norma Farnes and Susan
Hatt-Cook, both untiring supporters,
and Peter Windett who suffered the design
problems.
    We would also like to say how
impressed we are that all the
contributors who said they couldn't
draw were brave enough and cared
enough to have a go. The result is a
wealth of charm, inventiveness and
wit from all of them.

    We would also like to express our
thanks to the following people who,
due to one reason or another, could not
produce a drawing but nevertheless
wished the book every success.

Edmund Blunden
The Countess of Dartmouth, GLC
Frankie Howerd
Glenda Jackson
Sir Michael Tippett
Prof. Dr Konrad Lorenz
David Attenborough
The Prince Bernard of the Netherlands
Rolf Harris
Val Doonican
Lord and Lady Montagu
Pete Murray
Donald Swann
Clement Freud
Ronnie Corbett
Ingrid Bergman
Jack Brabham
Jilly Cooper
Sir Noel Coward
Marty Feldman
Christopher Logue
David Shepherd
David Dimbleby
Rt. Hon. Harold Wilson, MP
Denis Norden

The Elephant
by the Rt Hon Peter Walker, MBE, MP.

I am a mammal who lived in days past
Who discovered that I was the last
To inhabit the scenery
And eat all the greenery
Of Britain – and I was aghast.

Extinction's so boring, I find
And its really extremely unkind
There's no chance of breeding
So I'll just keep on feeding
And get my Will ordered and signed.

I gather that somewhere abroad
There's a gradually increasing horde
Of creatures like I
Not so big and more shy
But in jungle terms they are the lord.

So I bequeath them an area stark
If they find a spare place on the Ark
Just get Noah to agree
And you should always see
An elephant in Regents Park.

Poem chosen by Dame Sybil Thorndike

'Little Things'

   Little things that run and fail
And die in silence and despair.
Little things that fight and fail and fall
On earth and sea and air.
All trapt and frightened little things
The Mouse, the Coney, hear our prayer.
As we forgive those done to us
The Lamb, the Linnet and the Hare
Forgive us all our trespasses
Little creatures everywhere.

   James Stephens

'Little Things' from *The Collected Poems of James Stephens*
is reproduced by kind permission of
Mrs Iris Wise and MacMillan, London and Basingstoke.

CONTRIBUTORS

Kenneth Allsop 70
Eamonn Andrews 29
Anon 84
Viscount Bangor 110
Viscountess Bangor 110
Ronnie Barker 46
Marquess of Bath 79
Duke of Bedford 75
Michael Bentine 33
Ursula Bloom 42
Reginald Bosanquet 71
Benjamin Britten 62
Russell Brockbank 94
Lord George Brown 88
Max Bygraves 54
James Cameron 41
Barbara Cartland 39
Sir Hugh Casson 40
Leslie Charteris 80
Michael Chow 28
Peter Cook 42/43
Quentin Crewe 69
Robert Dougal 36/37
Lawrence Durrell 81
Barry Fantoni 73
Michael Flanders 93
Sir Vivian Fuchs 23
Andrew Gardner 49
Giles 5
Terry Gilliam 100
Robert Graves 99

Joyce Grenfell 19
Tony Hart 34
Laurence Harvey 90/91
Thor Heyerdahl 26
Jack Hobbs 66
Eric Hosking 107
Juliette Howard 25
Philip Howard 25
Roy Hudd 20/21
Richard Ingrams 55
Tony Jacklin 47
Hattie Jacques 48
Hon Mrs Michael Joseph 2
John Lennon 50
Richard Lester 57
Bernard Levin 22
Cyril Littlewood 103
Edward Lucie-Smith 56
Jack de Manio 87
Yehudi Menuhin 38
Keith Michel 92
Cliff Michelmore 61
Sir Bernard Miles 74
Spike Milligan 14/67/112
Dudley Moore 18
Kenneth More 109
Desmond Morris 82/83
Johnny Morris 63
Stirling Moss 27
Frank Muir 16
Sally Muir 100

Yoko Ono 51
Marjorie Proops 89
Sir Ralph Richardson 98
John Ridgway 108
William Rushton 96/97
Vidal Sassoon 58/59
Jimmy Savile 32
Peter Scott 68
Ronald Searle 64/65
Harry Secombe 24
Peter Sellers 17
Ned Sherrin 72
Alan Simpson 58/59
Sooty 86
Johnny Speight 111
Graham Stark 106
Ralph Steadman 30/31
Tom Stoppard 101
Noel Streatfeild 95
Roy Strong 102
Eric Sykes 60
Elizabeth Taylor 104/105
Dame Sybil Thorndike 7
Philip Toynbee 35
Rita Tushingham 76/77
Rt Hon Peter Walker MP 6
Lalla Ward 110
Arnold Wesker 44/45
Katherine Whitehorn 85
Kenneth Williams 78
Godfrey Winn 52/53

Spike Milligan obviously hopes that this book of pictures will encourage people to take a sympathetic interest in wildlife. I dearly hope he is right, provided only that people don't get so carried away by the charm and beauty of the creatures in the pictures that they feel badly let down when they see roughly similar animals in the flesh.

Publication and other problems mean that I am unable to look over all the contributions to this book before composing these few words of commendation. I can therefore only say that, whatever the contents, the book is in a good cause, so that anyone who buys it can indulge in a modest amount of satisfaction without even having to open it. The Wildlife Youth Service deserves all the help and encouragement it can get.

Having collected and displayed just how the great and the famous see their favourite animals, I think it would only be fair to compose a companion collection of drawings of their favourite people by the animals.

1971.

The Wildlife Youth Service tries to help children to take more interest in the preservation of Wildlife everywhere. Children, in fact, join in study projects which produce lots of useful observations on British Wildlife. Schools and education authorities work closely with the Youth Service. The children have a special fund-raising section called AID Corps which in five years has contributed nearly £60,000 to conservation projects all over the world.

In addition there is the PANDA Club for 5–10 year olds and the Wildlife Observers for 11–18 year olds. We organize camps, rambles, study projects, etc. and have our own magazine 'Wildlife Reporter' which is published as a supplement in *Animals*.

The Wildlife Youth Service is not necessarily out to recruit the keen 'young naturalist' type of child but to enrol every boy and girl who is in any way interested in wildlife, and who feels that it is worth preserving for the future.

Unfortunately it is too late to save some species but others can be saved now if people care enough.

All children like animals and if they can be taught to change this affection to real care for nature as they grow then the world has a chance of being more habitable in the future. We hope you agree.

Cyril Littlewood, MBE.
Director Wildlife Youth Service
Marston Court, Manor Road,
Wallington, Surrey

That's the lecture over folks. Now read on:

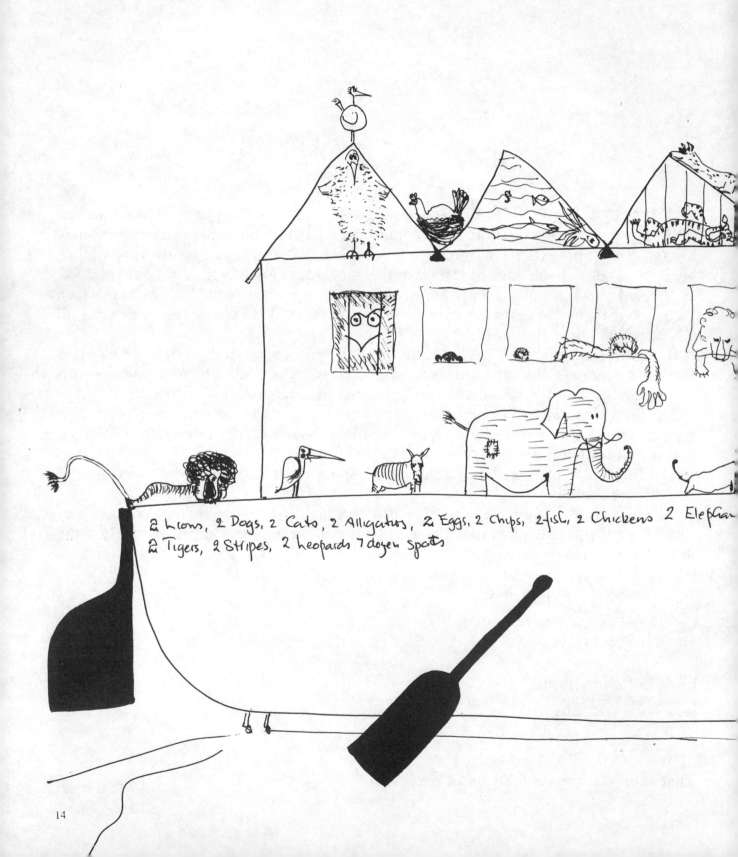

2 Lions, 2 Dogs, 2 Cats, 2 Alligators, 2 Eggs, 2 chips, 2 fish, 2 Chickens 2 Elephan
2 Tigers, 2 Stripes, 2 leopards 7 dozen spots

odo, 39ᴬARK

TO ALL WILDLIFE

Before I am permitted by the laws of nature to go to work on an egg, there is a tedious and distasteful course of action which I am obliged to pursue;
To wit - to woo.

Civil Service Heron

Dudley Moore's Earwig
Poem by Spike Milligan

The earwig
Of Dudley Moore

Appears at dawn
Or half past four
If you have ears that are
Bald large and big
Pray cover them up
With Dudley's earwig.

The Bumble Bee by Joyce Grenfell

The Bumble Bee is oddly wrought
Aerodynamically it ought
To find it quite impossible to rise
But Bumble Bees don't know the rule,
For Bumble Bees don't go to schule—
They flies.

Four Echidnas by Roy Hudd

FOUR ECHIDNAS GOT OUT OF THEIR CAR
AND WALKED UP A HILL LED BY PA
WHEN THEY GOT TO THE TOP
THEIR FATHER SAID 'STOP!'
'PLEASE DO NOT LEAN OVER TOO FAR'
'HOW FAR CAN WE LEAN?'
'YES, WHAT DO YOU MEAN?'
CRIED HIS CHILDREN 'OH SHOW US DEAR DA'
'NO FARTHER THAN THAT' SAID DAD – AND THEN
                              SPLAT!

HE JUST LAY – LOOKING UP – SHOUTING
                    'AAAARGH!'

Giraffe going past a window   Bear climbing up a tree

Sir Vivian Fuchs

A peripatetic penguin I,
Who flippers vainly twixt sea and sky,
In friendly contemplation on a floe
I watch the ships that come and go,
And wonder why?

They fish not; nor do they commune
With us, each other, or the moon.
So why do they come breaking in?
Polluting ice is quite a sin:
Be gone, and soon!

AARDVARK

The Aardvark's shape is a funny one,
And its character's hardly a sunny one.
But — no cause for alarm,
It will do you no harm;
For "aardvark" never killed any one.

The Piebald Palomino Mare
by Philip Howard

   This piebald palomino mare
(a breed that is extremely rare)
Comes trotting through a field of grass.
Fritillaries fly to watch her pass.
Couronnes de thym et de marjolaine
les Elfes joyeux dansent sur la plaine.
She does not stop to browse or smell
The Amaranth and Asphodel
Because she does not want to miss
Milligan's boat. The scribe of this
Was helped with words and coloured pen
By daughter Juliette aged ten.

Philip Howard

"My stupid son, you pollute the Earth!"

Thor Heyerdahl

Elephant running on the Ark
Stirling Moss

Confucius he say 'Man who get slipped disc ends up at bottom of chart'
Ed. Note

Michael Chow

Orbital Ducking Station by Eamonn Andrews

A bird never flew on a wing—
O'Casey said.
    But that was a while ago.
O'Casey's dead!

To Spike — it's catching. Eamonn Andrews.

Politica

Ralph STEADman.

umal

Ralph Steadman

Rare Species of British Bird by Jimmy Savile

A PERUVIAN BLOTTO

THE PERUVIAN BLOTTOS ARE RARER
THAN VICUNAS ALPACAS OR LLAMAS
THEY LIVE IN THE HIGHEST SIERRA
AND ONLY EAT FLANNEL PYJAMAS.

GROEDIPUS REX

Tony Hart

Philip Toynbee

What do you think you're sniffing at ?

Philip Toynbee

Robert Dougal

The Fiddle-Beetle by Yehudi Menuhin

I am the Fiddle-Beetle
I hum by night or day
By nature centripetal
I wing my own sweet way.

Yehudi Menuhin

A dog will come when he is called;
A cat will walk away.
A pekinese will do as he please,
Whatever you may say.

Barbara Cartland

Guest Owls
and
Hippopotamouse

Sir Hugh Casson

James Cameron

The only Animal I do admire is the Tortoise.
He doth not prance about nor solicit favours.
He preyeth not on his fellows.
He moveth with circumspection.
His sex life is enigmatic,
Yet his passion abideth, yea, unto an hundred years.
He getteth not a move on; he despiseth deadlines.
Truly his bearing is a Model to us all.

James Cameron   (from the Sanskrit.)

This is the now extinct Great (H)awk—
an Aristocratic bird that died of shame through dropping its H's.
Peter Cook

Ursula Bloom

We call him Sebastian
Anxious and cautious
With one eye upon us
On account of he's Jewish.

We can't leave without him
He bounces at strangers
With love and affection
And makes them embarrassed
On account of he's Jewish.

He licks them with relish
Though tired and harassed
He forces attention
But only for seconds
His joy's soon diminished
At which he collapses
On account of he's Jewish,

As long as you're near him
To hear and protect him
And feed him and need him
And smother and lather
His ears with affection
And give him attention
On account of he's Jewish.

Arnold Wesker

We can't leave without him
He bounces at strangers
With love and affection
And makes them embarrassed
On account of he's Jewish

As long as you're near him
To hear and protect him
And feed him and need him
And smother and lather
His ears with affection
And give him attention
On account of he's Jewish.

For Spike and self life and
conservation
    from Arnold Wesker May 1971.

Here we see a friendly lion,
Conversing with a mouse;
And just behind him, we can see
The lion's corner house.

When porcupines are
a little bit sickerly
They are not nearly
so blooming prickerly.

Hattie Jacques

Andrew Gardner

THE GREATER WOGGLY COMING IN TO LAND IN THE MATING SEASON

Tittenhurst Park,
Ascot, Berkshire.
Ascot 23022

Tittenhurst Park,
Ascot, Berkshire.
Ascot 23022

Tittenhurst Park,
Ascot, Berkshire.
Ascot 23022

Tittenhurst Park,
Ascot, Berkshire.
Ascot 23022

(1) J.L. 71.

John Lennon

50

Invisible Animals

do you like my
mustache?

Please
let me out
of your
closet

Yoko Ono

51

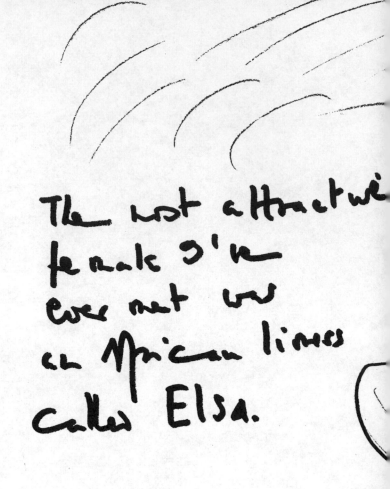

The most attractive
female I've
ever met was
an African lioness
called Elsa.

She seemed
most beautiful
of all, when she
turned her back!

Godfrey Winn

She seemed
most beautiful
of all, when she
turned her back!

I CANNOT DRAW AN ANIMAL
I DO NOT HAVE THE SKILL
SO I HAD TO SKETCH AN
OSTRICH
WHO DID'NT TAKE THE PILL

Max Bygraves.

Max Bygraves

PRIVATE EYE

34 Greek Street, London, W.1., 01-437 4017 Member of the Audit Bureau of Circulations

The Telephant

Richard Ingrams

Richard Ingrams

The pig exclaimed, on seeing the slicer,
'I think this world might well be nicer—

Which of us, should a vote be taken,
Would want to finish up as bacon?'

The slicer rasped, 'Now listen, pig!
Your brains are small; your bottom's big

This world is full of woe and waste—
Be grateful you're to someone's taste.'

Edward Lucie-Smith

The Pig by Edward Lucie-Smith

The pig exclaimed, on seeing the slicer,
'I think this world might well be nicer—

Which of us, should a vote be taken,
Would want to finish up as bacon?'

The slicer rasped, 'Now listen, pig!
Your brains are small; your bottom's big

This world is full of woe and waste—
Be grateful you're to someone's taste!'

The Roc

A
bird, now
understandably
extinct.

From an
Artist's impression, also extinct.

(Dick Lester)

The biggest snake in the world
having its dinner.
Alan Simpson

Vidal Sassoon

The long-tailed?

59

Eric Sykes

"Dear Eagle" said Miss Macalary,
"Whilst I live in auld Tipperary
    You live in an eyrie",
    The Eagle said, "Dearie,
I'd sooner live eyrie than therie."

Cliff Michelmore

Mich Clifflemouse
Doesn't live in a house
  He has no need to—
His mother had a big shoe
  Which she left him
  And it he now lives in,
With three other Clifflemouses.

May 13ᵗʰ 1971

THE RED HOUSE, ALDEBURGH, SUFFOLK.

Sorry – I's never been a draughtsman; the only things I have ever drawn have been fish, – comes of living by the North Sea I suppose

Benjamin Britten

Muriel, the Serval.

Muriel, a single Serval
Hoping to make things plural
Dreaming of several Servals
A Severval survival marvel.

Johnny Morris

Idiot horse under the impression that
it is representative of wild-life.

Ronald Searle ©

* See Miouw.

Spike Milligan

Social Climbing Penguin by Quentin Crewe

Social-climbing
Penguin

There are several kinds of animal whose habits I deplore,
I daresay I could make a list of twenty-eight or more.
It is not, you understand I hope, the simply graceless bunch,
Like the social-climbing penguin who wears a dinner-suit for lunch
Nor yet that dreadful monkey with his purple-coloured bum,
Nor those parrots, nor those mynahs, whose language shocks my Mum.
I am thinking of the spiders (and the stonefish, quicker still)
Which give you seven minutes in which to write your will.

There are mambas and mosquitoes and scorpions and cats,
Vultures, kreits and rattlesnakes, some flies and vampire bats.
Such killers, you might hazard, have evolved a simple plan:
The swift eradication of the species known as man.
Not so. In fact, more probable is exactly the reverse...
And if creatures are deplorable, then man is far, far worse.

Power to the Birds by Kenneth Allsop

Although Buzzards and Bustards are large
Pigeons and Wigeons are small . . .
Lesser Whitethroats and Lesser Kestrels,
Little Grebes, Little Owls, Little Gulls, Little Terns, Little Buntings,
Little Egrets . . .
Why this inferiority complex?
Why this lack of assertion among Twee-Sparrows, Dappers,
Dot-terels, Bit-terns, Cormo-runts, Half Pint-ails, Stunted Stints
and other avian Twiggies?
Let us think big, fowls everywhere!
Ignore the jeers and sneers of the counter-culture Vultures—
The Bearded Tits and the Whiskered Terns, the Black Terns
and the Rock Pipits, the Stoned Curlew and the Potridges.
Resist 'em!
Join the system!
Speed-up is needed in the bird herd.
For a change, let us prize size.
So we are about to build a runway extending from
Birmingham to Byfleet
For the bird who will make Foulness instantly obsolete:
S U P E R T I T

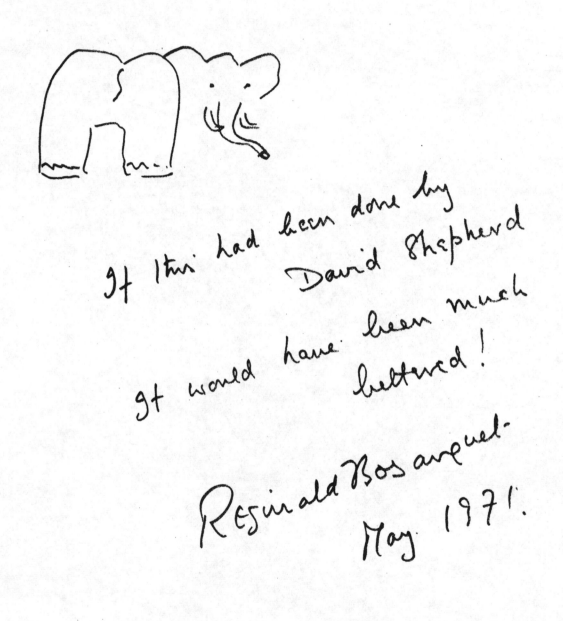

If this had been done by
David Shepherd
It would have been much
bettered!

Reginald Bosanquet
May 1971.

Reginald Bosanquet

BIRDS

Birds

Ned Sherrin

A HORS

Bartyfantoni.
age 3½ yrs

Barry Fantoni

THE BIRD WITH THE CUPBOARD IN ITS TAIL.

THE OOZULUM BIRD
A VERY PRACTICAL
CREATURE
COMPLETELY DECIMALIZED.

STABILISERS

one toffee
to lure him on.

Top
Speed
4 m.p.h.

Books

Light

Towel

Bed

Bath

Pottie

SKID.

BRAKE

WHEEL

Bowl of
weetabix.

Bernard Miles.
(Copyright!)

Sir Bernard Miles

Woburn Abbey, Bedfordshire - Woburn 666

The Duke of Bedford.

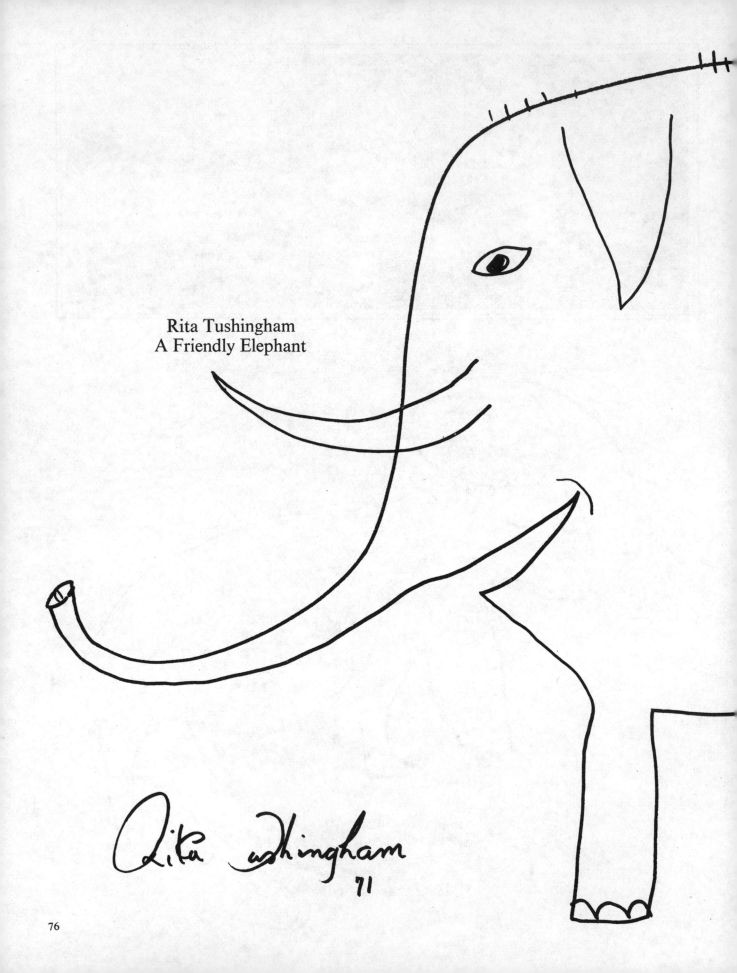

Rita Tushingham
A Friendly Elephant

Kenneth Williams

Kenneth Williams

This is a creature called 'SNIDE'
Whose endless pursuit of a bride
Was done all in vain
'Cos his NOSE in the rain
Would always stick out at the side.

The Marquess of Bath

The Hippo by Leslie Charteris

The Hippo is a ponderous beast
No gadabout, to say the least.
I wonder what the Freudian slip is
That got his name transferred to Hippies.

Leslie Charteris

study of a French tit vesting on it's laurels

Oscar Epfs
(Lawrence Durrell)

Lawrence Durrell

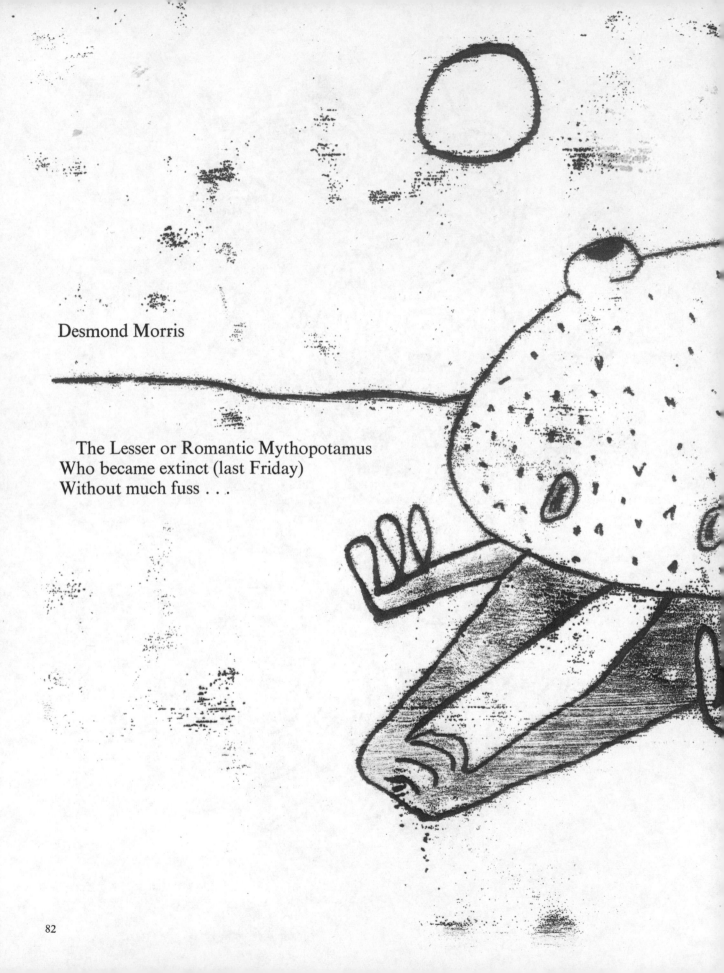

Desmond Morris

The Lesser or Romantic Mythopotamus
Who became extinct (last Friday)
Without much fuss . . .

82

The Gromet bird is short and fat
It lives on calories and that,
And finds it very hard to fly
When constructed like an apple pie.

The Gromet is a curious bird
And, in case you've never heard,
It lives in old abandoned socks
And flies around in odorous flocks,
Compelling those like you and me
To hold our nose and count to three.

The Gromet bird, as you may know,
Flies backwards to preserve a show
Of false white teeth and rubber hair –
All because its bottom's bare,
And no-one really wants to see
A sight like that before their tea.
Surely you will all agree?

Anon

The only objects I know how
To draw are these before you now.
    My pet—my vet—my set of creatures
Drawn sans eyes or other features
    Without removing pen from pad.
And if you think that you've been had
    And that they lack an eye, or grin,
Well, why don't *you* just fill them in?

Katherine Whitehorn

Katharine Whitehorn

A fearsum animal is man.
He wasn't here when the world began,
    But unless his aggreshun diminishes,
He'll be here when it finishes!

Sooty

by Sooty

4th June, 1971

Jack Hobbs, Esq.,
25 Bridge Street,
WALTON-ON-THAMES,
Surrey.

Dear Mr Hobbs

    Thank you for your letter inviting me to draw something for Milligan's Ark. Much as I admire Spike, I doubt if even he could decipher anything I drew so I will reluctantly decline and leave you with the following extract from my Memoirs to support my claim.

> Charlie Chaplin had lived close by the school and may well have been an earlier pupil there. Among my own contemporaries was Oscar Grasso, who later became famous as leader of Victor Sylvester's orchestra. Oscar was my rival for being top of the form – sometimes he would be top, sometimes I would be. He had one advantage over me, for he was quite good at drawing and I was hopeless at it. History and English were always my best subjects. But the school was keen on art and we had a notable art master in a man called Harold Thornton who fought hard to establish the importance of drawing in the curriculum. When it came to examinations he would give me 5 marks out of 100 for drawing, which meant that I had to do extremely well in other subjects to come top. Thornton was a great friend of John Evans, and he could never understand why Evans thought so highly of me when I was so useless in his art class.

Lord George Brown

(George Brown)

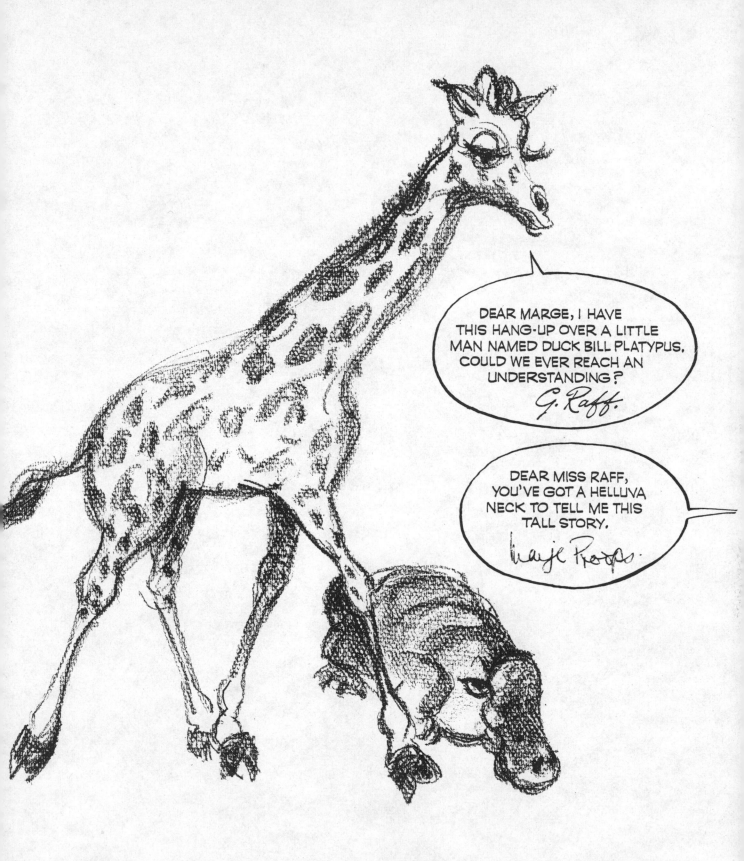

Marjorie Proops

As I look down at the earth
And crowded cities o'er which I fly;
No more that feeling of freedom,
No more a clear and unpolluted sky.
Knowing that I cannot shun
The hand of some inhuman gun
aimed at me from a smog filled
And destructive earth
Where millions seek to destroy
Each other and me from birth.

Laurence Harvey

Michell

Harold. a rather manly frog

Michael Flanders

I SOMETIMES THINK THE MODEST COD'S
THE ODDEST OF GOD'S ODDS AND SODS.

Michael Flanders

93

Italian Viper and Bertone's creature
I've not had the pleasure and don't wish to meet yer.

Brockbank

A camel has this proud expression
because he knows
that people only know 99
names for God,
whereas he knows the 100!
Noel Streatfeild

Noel Streatfeild

William Rushton

THE GLARB WAS A CONTENTED BEAST

BUT THEY USED ITS FEET FOR BREWER'S YEAST

AND ITS FUR MADE LOVELY BEDSIDE RUGS

AND ITS TEETH COULD BE TURNED INTO TASTEFUL JUGS

IT DIDN'T HAVE ARMS SO THEY COULDN'T USE THOSE

BUT ITS NOSE MADE YARDS OF GARDEN HOSE.

NOW THERE'S GLARBAL-TYPE RUGS, JUGS, HOSES AND BEERS

BUT YOU HAVEN'T SEEN A GLARB FOR A THOUSAND
                                    YEARS

The Poet Rushton

Here's a cat
On a mat
If you can believe that!

Sir Ralph Richardson

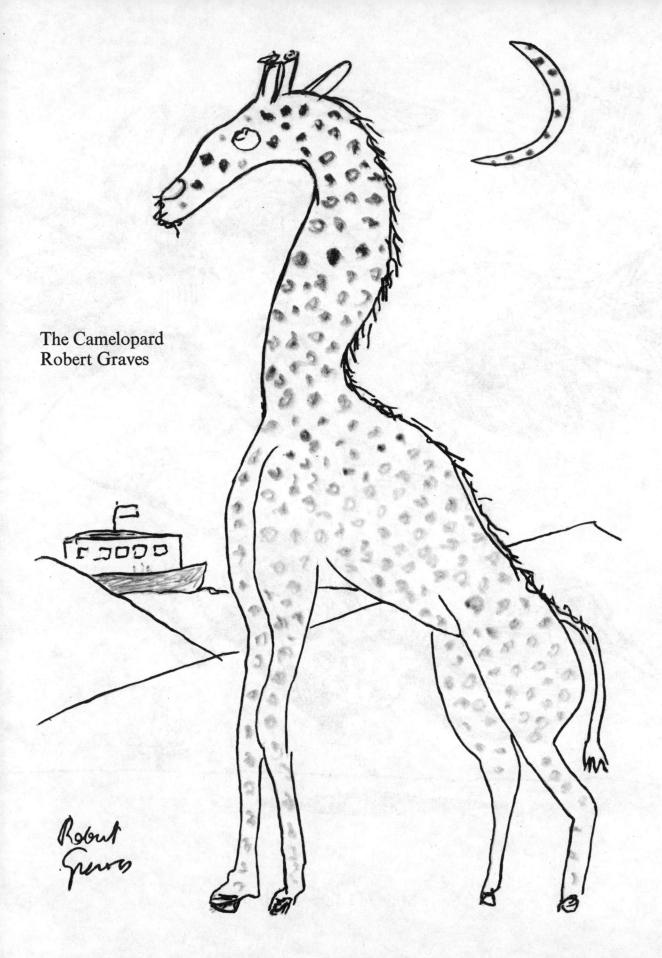

The Camelopard
Robert Graves

Robert Graves

Sally Muir and Terry Gilliam

ZEBRA (detail)

Tom Stoppard

'Crowned Crane' *Cranus McAlpinus*
(Builds massive concrete nests)

Sound of the sea, sea sounds
See the green white sea-smell
Taste the salt sweet spray
Hear the long lost sailors
In their unsweet bed.

See weed necklaces chained
To sand, sea animals
Sounding an everlasting silence.

Elizabeth Taylor ©

Sea Animal
by.
E. J. B.

THIS IS A KANGEROO.
WHO'S LEGS NUMBER ONLY TWO.
BUT IN HER POUCH
HER BABY DOES CROUCH
MAKING HER LEGS <u>FOUR</u> NOT TWO!

Graham Stark.

That is the last picture you will take'

Eric Hosking

The Puffin by John Ridgway

Its not much fun bein' a Puffin
they only think we're fit for stuffin!
far removed from cliffs and rocks
our feet glued to wooden blocks
stuck up on the mantlepiece
how the hell can we increase.
now what about our natural state?
you may well ask, the problem's great
the sea is mostly black, not blue
a seething mass of oily glue.
and as for radioactive fish
it's only fit for a suicide dish.
the air is filled with bits of lead,
and yet I've often heard it said
by those who seem to want us dead,
"how sad the Puffin's now so rare",
as if those fickle humans care!
to them our plight seems next to nuffin,
it's not much fun bein' a Puffin.

The Shrimp by Kenny More

A shrimp is a fish
or nearly so—
But does it have a mate?
I met a girl called Angela,
I met her on a 'date'
Now, ten years later,
she's my wife.
There's a funny thing,
A little shrimp, that's
almost a fish
Led to a wedding ring!

The Shark by Lalla Ward

  The shark
Swims
In the dark
Of the deep
Its eye gleams
As it sees
Streams
Of gold fish—
Bold fish
Swimming too near
For the shark is well aware
That here
Is a tasty dish
Of fish
And the shark lies
In wait—
No fisherman,
No flies
No bait.
And the fish swim past
The shark follows—
Fast,
And swallows.

Marjorie &
Edward Ward

Viscount and Viscountess Bangor

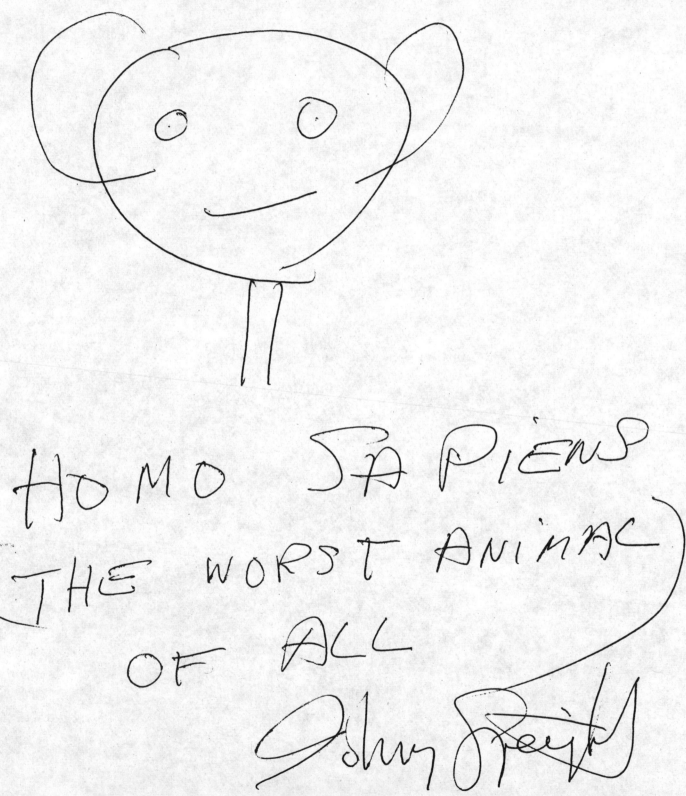

HOMO SAPIENS
(THE WORST ANIMAL
OF ALL)

Johnny Speight

Myxamatosis

Baby rabbits
With eyes full of pus
Is the work
Of scientific us.

Spike Milligan

'the Bookworm'